W9-CBC-394

COOL SPORTS
Surfing

Aaron Carr

AV2 BY WEIGL
MEDIA ENHANCED BOOKS
ADDED VALUE • AUDIO VISUAL

www.av2books.com

38888000177026

AV² provides enriched content that supplements and complements this book. Weigl's AV² books strive to create inspired learning and engage young minds in a total learning experience.

Your AV² Media Enhanced books come alive with...

Go to **www.av2books.com**, and enter this book's unique code.

BOOK CODE

J563282

AV² by Weigl brings you media enhanced books that support active learning.

Audio
Listen to sections of the book read aloud.

Video
Watch informative video clips.

Embedded Weblinks
Gain additional information for research.

Try This!
Complete activities and hands-on experiments.

Key Words
Study vocabulary, and complete a matching word activity.

Quizzes
Test your knowledge.

Slide Show
View images and captions, and prepare a presentation.

... and much, much more!

Published by AV² by Weigl
350 5th Avenue, 59th Floor, New York, NY 10118
Website: www.av2books.com   www.weigl.com

Library of Congress Cataloguing in Publication data available upon request.
Fax 1-866-449-3445 for the attention of the Publishing Records department.

ISBN 978-1-61913-515-4 (hard cover)
ISBN 978-1-61913-521-5 (soft cover)

Printed in the United States of America in North Mankato, Minnesota
3 4 5 6 7 8 9   17 16 15 14 13

062013
WEP240513

Editor: Aaron Carr   Art Director: Terry Paulhus

Weigl acknowledges Getty Images as the primary image supplier for this title.

COOL SPORTS

Surfing

CONTENTS

Surfing is a water sport. People use surfboards to ride on top of waves.

A surfboard is a long board that floats in water.
Most surfboards have a strap.
The strap helps keep the surfer and the board together.

Like a PRO

Pro surfers do many tricks with their surfboards.

Surfers often wear a wetsuit. This keeps them warm in cold water.

Like a PRO

Pro surfers put wax on their boards to keep from slipping.

9

People can surf in many places. Some people surf in oceans. Others surf in large lakes or rivers.

Like a PRO

Pro surfers ride in many different places.

Practice is important for anyone who wants to surf. It helps people become better at surfing.

Like a PRO

Pro surfers practice for many hours every day.

People do tricks, jumps, and turns on their surfboards. This is called Shortboard.

Like a PRO

Pro surfers get points for doing tricks in Shortboard.

When people surf for speed and style, it is called Longboard.

Like a PRO

Pro surfers still use moves from many years ago.

Surfers compete in many events all year. This is called the World Tour.

Like a PRO

Pro surfers earn points all year in World Tour.

Great surfers from all around the world compete for the ASP World Title.

Many people come to watch the surfers ride large waves and do big jumps.

SURFING FACTS

These pages provide detailed information that expands on the interesting facts found in this book. These pages are intended to be used by adults as a learning support to help young readers round out their knowledge of each sport in the *Cool Sports* series.

Pages 4–5

Surfing is a water sport. People use surfboards to ride on top of waves.

Surfers stand on a board and ride on top of waves. As the waves push the surfer toward the shore, the surfer rides sideways along the wave. Surfing is believed to have started in Polynesia between 1500 BC and 400 AD. The first surfers used long, heavy boards to ride the waves. Over time, surfing grew into a sport that requires strength, skill, and balance.

Pages 6–7

A surfboard is a long board that floats in water. Most surfboards have a strap. The strap helps keep the surfer and the board together.

Like a PRO

Pro surfers do many tricks with their surfboards.

There are many kinds of surfboards. Shortboards are usually about 6 feet (1.8 meters) long and very lightweight. These boards are often used for doing tricks. Longboards are usually about 10 feet (3 m) long. These boards are often used for more traditional types of surfing. Early Hawai'ian surfboards were made of wood, measured up to 25 feet (7.6 m) long, and weighed up to 200 pounds (91 kilograms). Today, many boards are made of lightweight foam.

Pages 8–9

Surfers often wear a wetsuit. This keeps them warm in cold water.

Like a PRO

Pro surfers put wax on their boards to keep from slipping.

Surfers should always wear a wetsuit when surfing in cold water. A wetsuit is a skin-tight suit that keeps the surfer warm. Wetsuits are made for different activities and have different thicknesses. It is important to choose a wetsuit that is well matched to the activity and the weather conditions. Waxing the board provides extra grip to keep the surfer on the board.

Pages 10–11

People can surf in many places. Some people surf in oceans. Others surf in large lakes or rivers.

Like a PRO

Pro surfers ride in many different places.

People can surf almost anywhere there is water and waves. Some of the most popular places to surf include the beaches of Hawai'i, Australia, California, and Florida, as well as the Great Lakes of North America and some rivers in Germany. Most surfing is done in shallow ocean water. This is where the biggest and most consistent waves are found.

Practice is the most important part of becoming a good surfer. It takes many hours of practice over a period of years to master the skills needed for surfing. Most professional surfers practice for many hours every day. They push themselves to master different types of waves and riding conditions. Professional surfers push themselves to learn new moves and improve their skills.

Shortboard surfing, or shortboarding, is one of the most common types of surfing. Shortboarding is done on a board between 6 and 7 feet (1.8 and 2 m) long. Shortboards are pointed at the front, either rounded or squared at the back, and have between two and five fins, or skegs. The short length and skegs make these boards faster and easier to control for difficult tricks and jumps.

Longboard surfing, or longboarding, is similar to traditional surfing. Longboards range from 9 to 12 feet (2.7 to 3.7 m) long, and they usually only have one skeg. Longboards are not as maneuverable as shortboards, so they are not suited to performing aerial tricks. However, longboards offer better balance than shortboards.

Each year, the Association of Surfing Professionals (ASP) World Tour determines the world's best surfers. The tour features the top-ranked surfers in the world competing in events throughout the year. Men compete in 10 events, and women compete in seven. The surfer with the most points at the end of the year is named the world champion.

The ASP began in 1976 as a way of determining a professional surfing world champion. The ASP World Tour is made up of several pro surfing events held around the world each year. Men and women who earn the most points in these competitions are named the world champions. The ASP has men's and women's events in shortboard and longboard.

KEY WORDS

Research has shown that as much as 65 percent of all written material published in English is made up of 300 words. These 300 words cannot be taught using pictures or learned by sounding them out. They must be recognized by sight. This book contains 63 common sight words to help young readers improve their reading fluency and comprehension. This book also teaches young readers several important content words. These words are paired with pictures to aid in learning and improve understanding.

Page	Sight Words First Appearance
4	a, is, of, on, people, to, use, water
6	and, have, helps, in, keep, long, most, that, the, together
7	do, like, many, their, with
8	often, them, this
9	put
10	can, large, or, others, places, rivers, some
11	different
12	at, for, good, important, wants, who
13	day, every
14	this
15	get, points
16	it, when
17	both, moves, new, old
18	all, world, year
19	add, up
21	around, big, come, from, great, watch

Page	Content Words First Appearance
4	sport, surfboards, surfing, waves
6	board, strap, surfer
7	pro, tricks
8	wetsuit
9	wax
10	lakes, oceans
12	practice
13	hours
14	jumps, Shortboard, turns
16	Longboard, speed, style
18	events, World Tour
21	ASP World Title